T0378332

Angel Reese

Published in the United States of America by Cherry Lake Publishing
Ann Arbor, Michigan
www.cherrylakepublishing.com

Reading Adviser: Beth Walker Gambro, MS, Ed., Reading Consultant, Yorkville, IL
Illustrator: Leo Trinidad

Photo Credits: © Sean Pavone/Shutterstock, 5; © matimix/Shutterstock, 7; © Natallya Naumava/Dreamstime.com; © tony quinn / Alamy Stock Photo; © Cal Sport Media/Alamy Stock Photo, 13, 22; © AP Photo/Mary Altaffer/ASSOCIATED PRESS; © Shaina Benhiyoun/SPP/Sipa USA via AP, 17, 23; Official White House Photo by Erin Scott, 19; © Melissa Tamez/Icon Sportswire via AP Images/ASSOCIATED PRESS, 21

Cherry Lake Press is an imprint of Cherry Lake Publishing Group

Library of Congress Cataloging-in-Publication Data has been filed and is available at catalog.loc.gov.

Printed in the United States of America

table of contents

About the author: When not writing, Dr. Virginia Loh-Hagan serves as the Executive Director for AANAPISI Affairs and the APIDA Center at San Diego State University. She is also the Co-Executive Director of The Asian American Education Project. She lives in San Diego with her very tall husband and very naughty dogs.

About the illustrator: Leo Trinidad is a *New York Times* bestselling comic book artist, illustrator, and animator from Costa Rica. For more than 12 years, he's been creating content for children's books and TV shows. Leo created the first animated series ever produced in Central America and founded Rocket Cartoons, one of the most successful animation studios in Latin America. He is also the 2018 winner of the Central American Graphic Novel contest.

I was born in 2002.

I was born in Maryland.

I loved playing sports. Basketball was my favorite.

My mother taught me.

Do you play any sports?

I played against my brother.

We played in our driveway.

I played in **leagues**. I played in high school. I was tall.

I was the best player.

I played in college. I went to Louisiana State. I won big games.

I was a champion.

What are you good at?

I look good on the court. I do my hair, makeup, and nails.

I was called the "**Bayou** Barbie."

I play **professional** women's basketball. I broke records.

I have many fans.

I am a role model. I support Black women.

I am proud of my skin.

My legacy lives on. I am **talented**.

I love who I am.

What would you like to ask me?

2022

1990

Born
2002

2024

2090

glossary

bayou (BIE-yoo) slow-moving waterway found in Louisiana and other southern states

leagues (LEEGZ) groups of sports teams that play against each other

professional (pruh-FESH-nuhl) related to a job; describing when someone is paid for their work

talented (TAA-luhnt-uhd) gifted or skilled

index